SELECTED POEMS OF
THOMAS HARDY

SELECTED POEMS OF
THOMAS HARDY
1840 –1928

METHUEN

This selection first published in Great Britain by Methuen 2005
Copyright © 2005 by Methuen Publishing Ltd

Methuen Publishing Ltd
215 Vauxhall Bridge Road
London SW1V 1EJ
www.methuen.co.uk

Methuen Publishing Limited Reg. No. 3543167

ISBN 0 413 77505 4

1 3 5 7 9 10 8 6 4 2

A CIP catalogue for this title
is available from the British Library.

Printed and bound in Great Britain
by St Edmundsbury Press, Bury St Edmunds, Suffolk

Contents

The Darkling Thrush

I LEANT upon a coppice gate
   When Frost was spectre-gray,
And Winter's dregs made desolate
   The weakening eye of day.
The tangled bine-stems scored the sky
   Like strings of broken lyres,
And all mankind that haunted nigh
   Had sought their household fires.

The land's sharp features seemed to be
   The Century's corpse outleant,
His crypt the cloudy canopy,
   The wind his death-lament.
The ancient pulse of germ and birth
   Was shrunken hard and dry,
And every spirit upon earth
   Seemed fevourless as I.

At once a voice arose among
   The bleak twigs overhead
In a full-hearted evensong
   Of joy illimited;
An aged thrush, frail, gaunt, and
   small,

blast-beruffled plume,
Had chosen thus to fling his soul
  Upon the growing gloom.

So little cause for carolings
  Of such ecstatic sound
Was written on terrestrial things
  Afar or nigh around,
That I could think there trembled through
  His happy good-night air
Some blessed Hope, whereof he knew
  And I was unaware.

Wessex Heights

THERE are some heights in Wessex, shaped as if by a kindly
hand
For thinking, dreaming, dying on, and at crises when I
stand,
Say, on Ingpen Beacon eastward, or on Wylls-Neck
westwardly,
I seem where I was before my birth, and after death may
be.

In the lowlands I have no comrade, not even the lone
man's friend –
Her who suffereth long and is kind; accepts what he is too
weak to mend:
Down there they are dubious and askance; there nobody
thinks as I,
But mind-chains do not clank where one's next neighbour
is the sky.

In the towns I am tracked by phantoms having weird
detective ways –
Shadows of beings who fellowed with myself of earlier
days:

They hang about at places, and they say harsh heavy
   things –
Men with a wintry sneer, and women with tart
   disparagings.

Down there I seem to be false to myself, my simple self
   that was,
And is not now, and I see him watching, wondering what
   crass cause
Can have merged him into such a strange continuator as
   this,
Who yet has something in common with himself, my
   chrysalis.

I cannot go to the great grey Plain; there's a figure against
   the moon,
Nobody sees it but I, and it makes my breast beat out of
   tune;
I cannot go to the tall-spired town, being barred by the
   forms now passed
For everybody but me, in whose long vision they stand
   there fast.

There's a ghost at Yell'ham Bottom chiding loud at the fall
   of the night,
There's a ghost in Froom-side Vale, thin lipped and vague,
   in a shroud of white,

There is one in the railway-train whenever I do not want it
near,
I see its profile against the pane, saying what I would not
hear.

As for one rare fair woman, I am now but a thought of
hers,
I enter her mind and another thought succeeds me that she
prefers;
Yet my love for her in its fulness she herself even did not
know;
Well, time cures hearts of tenderness, and now I can let her
go.

So I am found on Ingpen Beacon, or on Wylls-Neck to the
west,
Or else on homely Bulbarrow, or little Pilsdon Crest,
Where men have never cared to haunt, nor women have
walked with me,
And ghosts then keep their distance; and I know some
liberty.

Domicilium

Iт faces west, and round the back and sides
High beeches, bending, hang a veil of boughs,
And sweep against the roof. Wild honeysucks
Climb on the walls, and seem to sprout a wish
(If we may fancy wish of trees and plants)
To overtop the apple-trees hard by.

Red roses, lilacs, variegated box
Are there in plenty, and such hardy flowers
As flourish best untrained. Adjoining these
Are herbs and esculents; and farther still
A field; then cottages with trees, and last
The distant hills and sky.

Behind, the scene is wilder. Heath and furze
Are everything that seems to grow and thrive
Upon the uneven ground. A stunted thorn
Stands here and there, indeed; and from a pit
An oak uprises, springing from a seed
Dropped by some bird a hundred years ago.

                              In days bygone –
Long gone – my father's mother, who is now
Blest with the blest, would take me out to walk.
At such a time I once inquired of her
How looked the spot when first she settled here.
The answer I remember. 'Fifty years
Have passed since then, my child, and change has marked
The face of all things. Yonder garden-plots
And orchards were uncultivated slopes
O'ergrown with bramble bushes, furze and thorn:
That road a narrow path shut in by ferns,
Which, almost trees, obscured the passer-by.

'Our house stood quite alone, and those tall firs
And beeches were not planted. Snakes and efts
Swarmed in the summer days, and nightly bats
Would fly about our bedrooms. Heathcroppers
Lived on the hills, and were our only friends;
So wild it was when we first settled here.'

The Ruined Maid

'O 'MELIA, my dear, this does everything crown!
Who could have supposed I should meet you in Town?
And whence such fair garments, such prosperi-ty?' –
'O didn't you know I'd been ruined?' said she.

– 'You left us in tatters, without shoes or socks,
Tired of digging potatoes, and spudding up docks;
And now you've gay bracelets and bright feathers three!' –
'Yes: that's how we dress when we're ruined,' said she.

– 'At home in the barton you said "thee" and "thou",
And "thik oon", and "theäs oon", and "t'other"; but now
Your talking quite fits 'ee for high compa-ny!' –
'Some polish is gained with one's ruin,' said she.

– 'Your hands were like paws then, your face blue and
      bleak
But now I'm bewitched by your delicate cheek,
And your little gloves fit as on any la-dy!' –
'We never do work when we're ruined,' said she.

– 'You used to call home-life a hag-ridden dream,
And you'd sigh, and you'd sock; but at present you seem
To know not of megrims or melancho-ly!' –
'True. One's pretty lively when ruined,' said she.

– 'I wish I had feathers, a fine sweeping gown,
And a delicate face, and could strut about Town!' –
'My dear – a raw country girl, such as you be,
Cannot quite expect that. You ain't ruined,' said she.

The Subalterns

I

'Poor wanderer,' said the leaden sky,
  'I fain would lighten thee,
But there are laws in force on high
  Which say it must not be.'

II

– 'I would not freeze thee, shorn one,' cried
  The North, 'knew I but how
To warm my breath, to slack my stride;
  But I am ruled as thou.'

III

– 'To-morrow I attack thee, wight,'
  Said Sickness. 'Yet I swear
I bear thy little ark no spite,
  But am bid enter there.'

IV

– 'Come hither, Son,' I heard Death say;
  'I did not will a grave
Should end thy pilgrimage to-day,
  But I, too, am a slave!'

V

We smiled upon each other then,
   And life to me had less
Of that fell look it wore ere when
   They owned their passiveness.

'Ah, Are You Digging on My Grave?'

'Ah, are you digging on my grave
   My loved one? – planting rue?'
– 'No: yesterday he went to wed
One of the brightest wealth has bred.
"It cannot hurt her now," he said,
   "That I should not be true."'

'Then who is digging on my grave?
   My nearest dearest kin?'
– 'Ah, no: they sit and think, "What use!
What good will planting flowers produce?
No tendance of her mound can loose
   Her spirit from Death's gin."'

'But someone digs upon my grave?
   My enemy? – prodding sly?'
– 'Nay: when she heard you had passed the Gate
That shuts on all flesh soon or late,
She thought you no more worth her hate,
   And cares not where you lie.'

'Then, who is digging on my grave?
   Say – since I have not guessed!'
– 'O it is I, my mistress dear,
Your little dog , who still lives near,
And much I hope my movements here
   Have not disturbed your rest?'

'Ah yes! *You* dig upon my grave ...
   Why flashed it not on me
That one true heart was left behind !
What feeling do we ever find
To equal among human kind
   A dog's fidelity!'

'Mistress, I dug upon your grave
   To bury a bone, in case
I should be hungry near this spot
When passing on my daily trot.
I am sorry, but I quite forgot
   It was your resting place.'

Channel Firing

THAT night your great guns, unawares,
Shook all our coffins as we lay,
And broke the chancel window-squares,
We thought it was the Judgment-day

And sat upright. While drearisome
Arose the howl of wakened hounds:
The mouse let fall the altar-crumb,
The worms drew back into the mounds,

The glebe cow drooled. Till God cried, 'No;
It's gunnery practice out at sea
Just as before you went below;
The world is as it used to be:

'All nations striving strong to make
Red war yet redder. Mad as hatters
They do no more for Christés sake
Than you who are helpless in such matters.

'That this is not the judgment-hour
For some of them's a blessed thing,
For if it were they'd have to scour
Hell's floor for so much threatening ...

'Ha, ha. It will be warmer when
I blow the trumpet (if indeed
I ever do; for you are men,
And rest eternal sorely need).'

So down we lay again. 'I wonder,
Will the world ever saner be,'
Said one, 'than when He sent us under
In our indifferent century!'

And many a skeleton shook his head.
'Instead of preaching forty year,'
My neighbour Parson Thirdly said,
'I wish I had stuck to pipes and beer.'

Again the guns disturbed the hour,
Roaring their readiness to avenge,
As far inland as Stourton Tower,
And Camelot, and starlit Stonehenge.

The Convergence of the Twain

(Lines on the loss of the 'Titanic')

I

In a solitude of the sea
Deep from human vanity,
And the Pride of Life that planned her, stilly couches she.

II

Steel chambers, late the pyres
Of her salamandrine fires,
Cold currents thrid, and turn to rhythmic tidal lyres.

III

Over the mirrors meant
To glass the opulent
The sea-worm crawls – grotesque, slimed, dumb,
                    indifferent.

IV

Jewels in joy designed
To ravish the sensuous mind
Lie lightless, all their sparkles bleared and black and blind.

V

Dim moon-eyed fishes near

Gaze at the gilded gear

And query: 'What does this vaingloriousness down

here?'

VI

Well: while was fashioning

This creature of cleaving wing,

The Immanent Will that stirs and urges everything

VII

Prepared a sinister mate

For her – so gaily great –

A Shape of Ice, for the time far and dissociate.

VIII

And as the smart ship grew

In stature, grace, and hue,

In shadowy silent distance grew the Iceberg too.

IX

Alien they seemed to be:

No mortal eye could see

The intimate welding of their later history,

X

Or sign that they were bent
By paths coincident
On being anon twin halves of one august event,

XI

Till the Spinner of the Years
Said 'Now!' And each one hears,
And consummation comes, and jars two hemispheres.

The Recalcitrants

Let us off and search, and find a place
Where yours and mine can be natural lives,
Where no one comes who dissects and dives
And proclaims that ours is a curious case,
Which its touch of romance can scarcely grace.

You would think it strange at first, but then
Everything has been strange in its time.
When some one said on a day of the prime
He would bow to no brazen god again
He doubtless dazed the mass of men.

None will see in us a pair whose claims
To righteous judgment we care not making;
Who have doubted if breath be worth the taking,
And have no respect for the current fames
Whence the savour has flown while abide the names.

We have found us already shunned, disdained,
And for re-acceptance have not once striven;
Whatever offence our course has given
The brunt thereof we have long sustained.
Well, let us away, scorned, unexplained.

The Last Signal
(Oct. 11, 1886)
A memory of William Barnes

SILENTLY I footed by an uphill road
That led from my abode to a spot yew-boughed;
Yellowly the sun sloped low down to westward,
    And dark was the east with cloud.

Then, amid the shadow of that livid sad east,
    Where the light was least, and a gate stood wide,
Something flashed the fire of the sun that was facing it,
    Like a brief blaze on that side.

Looking hard and harder I knew what it meant –
    The sudden shine sent from the livid east scene;
It meant the west mirrored by the coffin of my friend
       there,
    Turning to the road from his green,

To take his last journey forth – he who in his prime
    Trudged so many a time from that gate athwart the
       land!
Thus a farewell to me he signalled on his grave-way,
    As with a wave of his hand.

Transformations

Portion of this yew
Is a man my grandsire knew,
Bosomed here at its foot:
This branch may be his wife,
A ruddy human life
Now turned to a green shoot.

These grasses must be made
Of her who often prayed,
Last century, for repose;
And the fair girl long ago
Whom I often tried to know
May be entering this rose.

So, they are not underground,
But as nerves and veins abound
In the growths of upper air,
And they feel the sun and rain,
And the energy again
That made them what they were!

Heredity

I AM the family face;
Flesh perishes, I live on,
Projecting trait and trace
Through time to times anon,
And leaping from place to place
Over oblivion.

The years-heired feature that can
In curve and voice and eye
Despise the human span
Of durance – that is I;
The eternal thing in man,
That heeds no call to die

The Self-Unseeing

HERE is the ancient floor,
Footworn and hollowed and thin,
Here was the former door
Where the dead feet walked in.

She sat here in her chair,
Smiling into the fire;
He who played stood there,
Bowing it higher and higher.

Childlike, I danced in a dream;
Blessings emblazoned that day;
Everything glowed with a gleam;
Yet we were looking away!

The Torn Letter

I

I TORE your letter into strips
  No bigger than the airy feathers
  That ducks preen out in changing weathers
Upon the shifting ripple-tips.

II

In darkness on my bed alone
  I seemed to see you in a vision,
  And hear you say: 'Why this derision
Of one drawn to you, though unknown?'

III

Yes, eve's quick mood had run its course,
  The night had cooled my hasty madness;
  I suffered a regretful sadness
Which deepened into real remorse.

IV

I thought what pensive patient days
  A soul must know of grain so tender,
  How much of good must grace the sender
Of such sweet words in such bright phrase.

V

Uprising then, as things unpriced
  I sought each fragment, patched and mended;
  The midnight whitened ere I had ended
And gathered words I had sacrificed.

VI

But some, alas, of those I threw
  Were past my search, destroyed for ever:
  They were your name and place; and never
Did I regain those clues to you.

VII

I learnt I had missed, by rash unheed,
  My track; that, so the Will decided,
  In life, death, we should be divided,
And at the sense I ached indeed.

VIII

That ache for you, born long ago,
  Throbs on; I never could outgrow it.
  What a revenge, did you but know it!
But that, thank God, you do not know.

The Voice

Woman much missed, how you call to me, call to me,
Saying that now you are not as you were
When you had changed from the one who was all to me,
But as at first, when our day was fair.

Can it be you that I hear? Let me view you, then,
Standing as when I drew near to the town
Where you would wait for me: yes, as I knew you then,
Even to the original air-blue gown!

Or is it only the breeze in its listlessness
Travelling across the wet mead to me here,
You being ever dissolved to wan wistlessness,
Heard no more again far or near?

    Thus I; faltering forward,
    Leaves around me falling,
Wind oozing thin through the thorn from norward,
    And the woman calling.

The Phantom Horsewoman

I

QUEER are the ways of a man I know:
        He comes and stands
        In a careworn craze,
        And looks at the sands
        And in the seaward haze
        With moveless hands
        And face and gaze,
        Then turns to go ...
And what does he see when he gazes so?

II

They say he sees as an instant thing
        More clear than to-day,
        A sweet soft scene
        That once was in play
        By that briny green;
        Yes, notes alway
        Warm, real, and keen,
        What his back years bring –
A phantom of his own figuring.

III

Of this vision of his they might say more:

    Not only there

    Does he see this sight,

    But everywhere

    In his brain – day, night,

    As if on the air

    It were drawn rose bright –

    Yea, far from that shore

Does he carry this vision of heretofore:

IV

A ghost-girl-rider. And though, toil-tried,

    He withers daily,

    Time touches her not,

    But she still rides gaily

    In his rapt thought

    On that shagged and shaly

    Atlantic spot,

    And as when first eyed

Draws rein and sings to the swing of the tide.

The Spell of
the Rose

'I MEAN to build a hall anon,
　　And shape two turrets there,
　　And a broad newelled stair,
And a cool well for crystal water;
　　Yes; I will build a hall anon,
　　Plant roses love shall feed upon,
　　And apple-trees and pear.'

He set to build the manor-hall,
　　And shaped the turrets there,
　　And the broad newelled stair,
And the cool well for crystal water;
　　He built for me that manor-hall,
　　And planted many trees withal,
　　But no rose anywhere.

And as he planted never a rose
　　That bears the flower of love,
　　Though other flower's throve
Some heart-bane moved our souls to sever
　　Since he had planted never a rose;
　　And misconceits raised horrid shows,
　　And agonies came thereof.

The Spell of the Rose

'I'll mend these miseries,' then said I,
     And so, at dead of night,
     I went and, screened from sight,
That nought should keep our souls in severance,
     I set a rose-bush. 'This,' said I,
     'May end divisions dire and wry,
          And long-drawn days of blight.'

But I was called from earth – yea, called
     Before my rose-bush grew;
     And would that now I knew
What feels he of the tree I planted,
     And whether, after I was called
To be a ghost, he, as of old,
          Gave me his heart anew!

Perhaps now blooms that queen of trees
     I set but saw not grow,
     And he, beside its glow –
Eyes couched of the mis-vision that blurred me –
     Ay, there beside that queen of trees
     He sees me as I was, though sees
          Too late to tell me so!

Going and Staying

I

THE moving sun-shapes on the spray,
The sparkles where the brook was flowing,
Pink faces, plightings, moonlit May,
These were the things we wished would stay;
    But they were going.

II

Seasons of blankness as of snow,
The silent bleed of a world decaying,
The moan of multitudes in woe,
These were the things we wished would go;
    But they were staying.

III

Then we looked closelier at Time,
And saw his ghostly arms revolving
To sweep off woeful things with prime,
Things sinister with things sublime
    Alike dissolving.

Weathers

I

THIS is the weather the cuckoo likes,
     And so do I;
When showers betumble the chestnut spikes,
     And nestlings fly;
And the little brown nightingale bills his best,
And they sit outside at 'The Traveller's Rest',
And maids come forth sprig-muslin drest,
And citizens dream of the south and west,
     And so do I.

II

This is the weather the shepherd shuns,
     And so do I;
When beeches drip in browns and duns,
     And thresh, and ply;
And hill-hid tides throb, throe on throe,
And meadow rivulets overflow,
And drops on gate-bars hang in a row,
And rooks in families homeward go,
     And so do I.

Afterwards

When the Present has latched its postern behind my
    tremulous stay,
  And the May month flaps its glad green leaves like
    wings,
Delicate-filmed as new-spun silk, will the neighbours say,
  'He was a man who used to notice such things'?

If it be in the dusk when, like an eyelid's soundless blink,
  The dewfall-hawk comes crossing the shades to alight
Upon the wind-warped upland thorn, a gazer may think,
  'To him this must have been a familiar sight.'

If I pass during some nocturnal blackness, mothy and
    warm,
  When the hedgehog travels furtively over the lawn,
One may say, 'He strove that such innocent creatures
    should come to no harm,
  But he could do little for them; and now he is gone.'

If, when hearing that I have been stilled at last, they stand
    at the door,
  Watching the full-starred heavens that winter sees,

Will this thought rise on those who will meet my face no
    more,
  'He was one who had an eye for such mysteries'?

And will any say when my bell of quittance is heard in the
    gloom,
  And a crossing breeze cuts a pause in its outrollings,
Till they rise again, as they were a new bell's boom,
  'He hears it not now, but used to notice such things'?'

Overlooking
the River Stour

THE swallows flew in the curves of an eight
    Above the river-gleam
    In the wet June's last beam:
Like little crossbows animate
The swallows flew in the curves of an eight
    Above the river-gleam.

Planing up shavings of crystal spray
    A moor-hen darted out
    From the bank thereabout,
And through the stream-shine ripped his way;
Planing up shavings of crystal spray
    A moor-hen darted out.

Closed were the kingcups; and the mead
    Dripped in monotonous green,
    Though the day's morning sheen
Had shown it golden and honeybee'd;
Closed were the kingcups; and the mead
    Dripped in monotonous green.

And never I turned my head, alack,
      While these things met my gaze
      Through the pane's drop-drenched glaze,
To see the more behind my back ...
O never I turned, but let, alack,
      These less things hold my gaze!

Fetching Her

An hour before the dawn,
       My friend,
You lit your waiting bedside-lamp,
Your breakfast-fire anon,
And outing into the dark and damp
You saddled, and set on.

Thuswise, before the day,
       My friend,
You sought her on her surfy shore,
To fetch her thence away
Unto your own new-builded door
For a staunch lifelong stay.

You said: 'It seems to be,
       My friend,
That I were bringing to my place
The pure brine breeze, the sea,
The mews – all her old sky and space,
In bringing her with me!'

– But time is prompt to expugn,
          My friend,
Such magic-minted conjurings:
The brought breeze fainted soon,
And then the sense of seamews' wings,
And the shore's sibilant tune.

So, it had been more due,
          My friend,
Perhaps, had you not pulled this flower
From the craggy nook it knew,
And set it in an alien bower;
But left it where it grew!

The Man He Killed

'Had he and I but met
 By some old ancient inn,
We should have set us down to wet
 Right many a nipperkin!

 'But ranged as infantry,
 And staring face to face,
I shot at him as he at me,
 And killed him in his place.

 'I shot him dead because –
 Because he was my foe,
Just so: my foe of course he was;
 That's clear enough; although

 'He thought he'd 'list, perhaps,
 'Off-hand like – just as I –
Was out of work – had sold his traps –
 No other reason why.

'Yes; quaint and curious war is!
You shoot a fellow down
You'd treat if met where any bar is,
Or help to half-a-crown.'